Yo Mama Jokes

300+ of the Funniest Yo Mama Jokes on Earth

Jimmy Joker

ISBN-13: 978-1534738348
ISBN-10: 1534738347

DEDICATION

This book is dedicated to anyone that enjoys a good laugh. Laughter is the best medicine and can cure any case of the "grumpies". Comedy and humor are the best and easiest way to make friends, create bonds, and share fun with others.

CONTENTS

Yo mama is so skinny...

Yo mama is so skinny... she looks just like a blow pop!

Yo mama is so skinny... she swallowed a meatball and thought she was pregnant.

Yo mama is so skinny... she has to wear a belt with her spandex pants.

Yo mama is so skinny... she hula hoops with a Cheerio.

Yo mama is so skinny... she has to run around in the shower just to get wet.

Yo mama is so skinny... she can hang glide with a Dorito!

Yo mama is so skinny... her bra fits better backwards.

Yo mama is so skinny... she uses cotton balls as a pillow.

Yo mama is so skinny... she can dive through a chain-linked fence.

Yo mama is so skinny... she can dodge rain drops!

Yo mama is so skinny... she turned sideways and disappeared.

Yo mama is so skinny... she don't get wet when it rains.

Yo mama is so skinny... her nipples touch.

Yo mama is so skinny... her pants have one belt loop!

Yo mama is so skinny... when she wears skinny jeans, they look like bell-bottoms!

Yo mama is so skinny... when she wore a yellow dress she looked like a pencil.

Yo mama is so skinny... she looks like a microphone stand!

Yo mama is so skinny... she can see through peepholes with both eyes.

Yo mama is so skinny... she uses cotton balls for pillows.

Yo mama is so fat...

Yo mama is so fat... she sat on a tractor and made a pick-up truck.

Yo mama is so fat... when she dives into the ocean there is a tsunami-warning!

Yo mama is so fat... she jumped in the air and got stuck.

Yo mama is so fat... when she took her shirt off at the strip club, everyone thought she was Jabber the Hut from Star Wars.

Yo mama is so fat... when she was in school she sat next to everybody!

Yo mama is so fat... when she turns around they throw her a welcome back party.

Yo mama is so fat... she sank the Titanic!

Yo mama is so fat... when she sits on the beach, whales swim up to her and sing, "We are family!"

Yo mama is so fat... she's got to wake up in sections.

Yo mama is so fat... she is on both sides of the family!

Yo mama is so fat... when she steps on the scale it says we don't do livestock.

Yo mama is so fat... when she goes to an amusement park, people try to ride her!

Yo mama is so fat... she gives herself group hugs!

Yo mama is so fat... she looks like she's smuggling an SUV!

Yo mama is so fat... when she plays hopscotch, she goes North America, South America, Europe, Asia.

Yo mama is so fat... NASA has to orbit a satellite around her!

Yo mama is so fat... when she steps on a scale, it read, "One at a time, please".

Yo mama is so fat... every time she walks in high heels, she strikes oil!

Yo mama is so fat... when she bungee jumps she goes straight to hell!

Yo mama is so fat... she rolled over four quarters and made a dollar!

Yo mama is so fat... the back of her neck is like a pack of hot dogs!

Yo mama is so fat... she posted a picture on Instagram and it crashed!

Yo mama is so fat... whenever she goes to the beach the tide comes in!

Yo mama is so fat... her blood type is gravy!

Yo mama is so fat... she's got her own area code!

Yo mama is so fat... when she lays on the beach no one else gets sun!

Yo mama is so fat... the highway patrol made her wear "Caution! Wide Turn!"

Yo mama is so fat... when she takes a bath she fills the tub then turns on the water.

Yo mama is so fat... she walked in front of the TV and I missed four shows.

Yo mama is so fat... she ate an entire pizza..... Hut!

Yo mama is so fat... she makes a whale look bulimic!

Yo mama is so fat... she jumped off the Grand Canyon and got stuck.

Yo mama is so fat... she left the house in high heels and came home in flip flops.

Yo mama is so fat... she sat on a rainbow and made Skittles.

Yo mama is so fat... her husband has to stand up in bed each morning to see if it's daylight!

Yo mama is so fat... she sat on an iPhone and turned it into an iPad!

Yo mama is so fat... she fell and made the Grand Canyon!

Yo mama is so fat... when she bungee jumps, she brings down the bridge too.

Yo mama is so fat... she was going to Wal-Mart, tripped over Kmart, and landed right on Target!

Yo mama is so fat... it took me a bus and two trains just to get on her good side.

Yo mama is so fat... when she has wants someone to shake her hand, she has to give directions!

Yo mama is so fat... that when she wanted a waterbed, they had to put a cover over the Pacific Ocean.

Yo mama is so fat... that she needs a bookmark to keep track of all her chin rolls!

Yo mama is so fat... when she wears a red dress all the kids scream look it's the Kool-Aid man.

Yo mama is so fat... the last time she saw 90210, it was on the scale!

Yo mama is so fat... when you go around her you get lost!

Yo mama is so fat... she uses an air balloon for a parachute.

Yo mama is so fat... she was floating in the ocean and Spain claimed her for the new world!

Yo mama is so fat... when she jumps up in the air she gets stuck!

Yo mama is so fat... when she lies on the beach people run around yelling "Free Willy!"

Yo mama is so fat... she put on her lipstick with a paint roller.

Yo mama is so fat... she goes to a restaurant, looks at the menu, and says, "Okay!"

Yo mama is so fat... you could use her bellybutton as a wishing well.

Yo mama is so fat... people jog around her for exercise.

Yo mama is so fat... she has seat belts on the chairs to keep her fat from rolling off!

Yo mama is so fat... she had to be baptized at sea world.

Yo mama is so fat... she went to the movies and sat next to everyone.

Yo mama is so fat... she eats Wheat Thicks.

Yo mama is so fat... when a bus hit her she said, "Who threw a pebble?"

Yo mama is so fat... when she goes to Taco Bell, they run for the border!

Yo mama is so fat... she has more chins than a Chinese phone book.

Yo mama is so fat... she broke a branch in her family tree!

Yo mama is so fat... when she wore a blue and green sweater, everyone thought she was planet Earth.

Yo mama is so fat... when she puts on her yellow rain coat and walks down the street people shout out "Taxi"!

Yo mama is so fat... she uses the interstate as a slip and slide.

Yo mama is so fat... she rolled out of bed and everybody thought there was an earthquake.

Yo mama is so fat... when God said, "Let there be light," he had to ask her to move out of the way.

Yo mama is so fat... they had to install speed bumps at all you can eat buffets.

Yo mama is so fat... when she went bungee jumping in a yellow dress everyone was screaming the suns falling!

Yo mama is so fat... she had her ears pierced by harpoon.

Yo mama is so fat... she needs a watch on both arms because she covers two time zones.

Yo mama is so fat... her measurements are 26-34-28, and her other arm is just as big!

Yo mama is so fat... the government forced her to wear taillights and blinkers so no one else would get hurt.

Yo mama is so fat... when she gets on the elevator it says, "Next stop, Hell"!

Yo mama is so fat... she supplies 99% of the world's gas.

Yo mama is so fat... she makes Godzilla look like an action figure.

Yo mama is so fat... her nickname is Lardo.

Yo mama is so fat... when her cell phone rings, people think she is backing up.

Yo mama is so fat... all she wanted for Christmas was to see her feet!

Yo mama is so fat... She went to Burger King, tripped over McDonald's, and landed on Wendy's!

Yo mama is so old...

Yo mama is so old... she used to babysit Adam and Eve!

Yo mama is so old... her memory is in black and white!

Yo mama is so old... she has a picture of Moses in her yearbook.

Yo mama is so old... that when she was in school there was no history class.

Yo mama is so old... her social security number is 1!

Yo mama is so old... she knew the Dead Sea when it started getting sick!

Yo mama is so old... she helped serve the Last Supper!

Yo mama is so old... she dated George Washington!

Yo mama is so old... she has an autographed Bible!

Yo mama is so old... she knew Burger King while he was still a prince.

Yo mama is so old... her first pet was a T-Rex!

Yo mama is so old... she was wearing a Jesus starter jacket!

Yo mama is so old... she farts dust!

Yo mama is so old... she knew the Great Wall of China when it was only good!

Yo mama is so old... she ran track with dinosaurs.

Yo mama is so old... she took her driving test on a dinosaur!

Yo mama is so old... her birth certificate says expired on it.

Yo mama is so old... that her bus pass is in hieroglyphics!

Yo mama is so old... her birth certificate is in Roman numerals.

Yo mama is so old... I told her to act her own age, and she died.

Yo mama is so old... she knew Mr. Clean when he had a head full of hair!

Yo mama is so old... I took a picture of her and it came out black and white!

Yo mama is so short...

Yo mama is so short ... she can walk under the door!

Yo mama is so short... she can sit on a dime and swing her legs.

Yo mama is so short... she does backflips under the bed.

Yo mama is so short... she has a job as a teller at a piggy bank.

Yo mama is so short ... she can play handball on the curb.

Yo mama is so short... she can use a sock for a sleeping bag.

Yo mama is so short ... she hangs out with the Keebler elves!

Yo mama is so short ... she's always the last person to know it's raining!

Yo mama is so short ... you can see her feet on her driver's license!

Yo mama is so short ... she can't roll dice – she has to push them!

Yo mama is so short ... she has to slam dunk her bus fare!

Yo mama is so short... she has to use rice to roll her hair up.

Yo mama is so short... she uses a toothpick as pool stick.

Yo mama is so short... she can tie her shoes while standing up.

Yo mama is so short ... she has to use a ladder to pick up a dime.

Yo mama is so short ... she drives a toy car!

Yo mama is so short ... she poses for trophies!

Yo mama is so short ... she broke her legs jumping off the toilet!

Yo mama is so short ... she drowned in a puddle!

Yo mama is so short... she can surf on a popsicle stick.

Yo mama is so tall...

Yo mama is so tall... she did a pushup and burned her neck on the sun!

Yo mama is so tall... she has to take a bath in the ocean.

Yo mama is so tall... she 69'd Bigfoot.

Yo mama is so tall... she can see her home from anywhere.

Yo mama is so tall... she tripped in Denver and hit her head in New York.

Yo mama is so tall... she did a cartwheel and kicked the gates of Heaven.

Yo mama is so tall... she tripped over a rock and hit her head on the moon.

Yo mama is so tall... Shaq looks up to her.

Yo mama is so tall... she did a cartwheel and kicked another planet!

Yo mama is so tall... she could use the Empire State Building as a toothpick!

Yo mama is so tall... Lisa Leslie is her mini-me!

Yo mama is so tall... she high-fived God.

Yo mama is so tall... she could use the Atlantic Ocean as a kiddy pool!

Yo mama is so tall... I can't stop seeing her!

Yo mama is so poor...

Yo mama is so poor... the last time she smelled a hot meal was when a rich man farted!

Yo mama is so poor... your family ate cereal with a fork to save milk.

Yo mama is so poor... she got caught stealing from Dollar General!

Yo mama is so poor... the roaches pay the light bill!

Yo mama is so poor... when it rains she says, "Shower time!"

Yo mama is so poor... thieves rob her house for practice!

Yo mama is so poor... she put a Happy Meal on layaway!

Yo mama is so poor... she was in K-Mart with a box of Hefty bags. I said, what are ya doing? She said, "Buying luggage."

Yo mama is so poor... birds throw bread at her!

Yo mama is so poor... it took her a year to save a penny!

Yo mama is so poor... a tornado hit her house and did a home improvement!

Yo mama is so poor... burglars break into her house and leave money!

Yo mama is so poor... her TV has two channels: ON and OFF!

Yo mama is so poor... her face is on a food stamp!

Yo mama is so poor... she can't even afford a Payday!

Yo mama is so poor... she drives a poor-shhh!

Yo mama is so poor... I jumped in a puddle and she scolded me for messing up her bath tub!

Yo mama is so poor... I stepped in her house and fell into the backyard.

Yo mama is so poor... she hangs toilet paper out to dry!

Yo mama is so poor... she waves around a popsicle stick and calls it air conditioning.

Yo mama is so poor... when I ring the doorbell she says, DING!

Yo mama is so poor... when her friend came over to use the bathroom she said, "Ok, choose a corner."

Yo mama is so poor... she can't afford to pay attention!

Yo mama is so poor... I walked in her house and stepped on a cigarette, and your mom said, "Who turned off the lights?"

Yo mama is so poor... when I saw her kicking a can down the street, I asked her what she was doing and she said, "Moving."

Yo mama is so ugly...

Yo mama is so ugly... people put pictures of her on their car to prevent theft!

Yo mama is so ugly... her mother had to be drunk to breast feed her!

Yo mama is so ugly... instead of putting the bungee cord around her ankle, they put it around her neck.

Yo mama is so ugly... when she joined an ugly contest, they said, "Sorry, no professionals."

Yo mama is so ugly... they had to feed her with a slingshot!

Yo mama is so ugly... that she scares blind people!

Yo mama is so ugly... when she walks into a bank they turn off the surveillance cameras.

Yo mama is so ugly... she looked in the mirror and her reflection committed suicide!

Yo mama is so ugly... even homeless people won't take her money!

Yo mama is so ugly... she's the reason blind dates were invented!

Yo mama is so ugly... they had to feed her with a Frisbee!

Yo mama is so ugly... when she watches TV the channels change themselves!

Yo mama is so ugly... she looked out the window and got arrested!

Yo mama is so ugly... she had to get a prescription mirror!

Yo mama is so ugly... bullets refuse to kill her!

Yo mama is so ugly... for Halloween she trick-or-treats on the phone!

Yo mama is so ugly... she looks like she has been bobbing for apples in hot grease!

Yo mama is so ugly... they passed a law saying she could only do online shopping!

Yo mama is so ugly... even a pit-bull wouldn't bite her!

Yo mama is so ugly... even Rice Krispies won't talk to her!

Yo mama is so ugly... that your father takes her to work with him so that he doesn't have to kiss her goodbye.

Yo mama is so ugly... she made the Devil go to church!

Yo mama is so ugly... she scares the paint off the wall!

Yo mama is so ugly... she scares roaches away!

Yo mama is so ugly... when she plays Mortal Kombat, Scorpion says, "Stay over there!"

Yo mama is so ugly... I told her to take out the trash and we never saw her again!

Yo mama is so ugly... she turned Medusa to stone!

Yo mama is so ugly... her pillow cries at night!

Yo mama is so ugly... she tried to take a bath and the water jumped out!

Yo mama is so ugly... even Hello Kitty said goodbye!

Yo mama is so ugly... she made an onion cry.

Yo mama is so ugly... when she walks down the street in September, people say "Wow, is it Halloween already?"

Yo mama is so ugly... she is the reason that Sonic the Hedgehog runs!

Yo mama is so ugly... The NHL banned her for life.

Yo mama is so ugly... when they took her to the beautician it took 24 hours for a quote!

Yo mama is so ugly... they didn't give her a costume when she tried out for Star Wars.

Yo mama is so ugly... just after she was born, her mother said, "What a treasure!" And her father said, "Yes, let's go bury it!"

Yo mama is so ugly... her mom had to tie a steak around her neck to get the dogs to play with her.

Yo mama is so ugly... she scared the crap out of a toilet!

Yo mama is so ugly... she gets 364 extra days to dress up for Halloween.

Yo mama is so ugly... she got beat up by her imaginary friends!

Yo mama is so ugly... the government moved Halloween to her birthday.

Yo mama is so stupid...

Yo mama is so stupid... when they said that it is chilly outside, she went outside with a bowl and a spoon.

Yo mama is so stupid... she tried to drown a fish!

Yo mama is so stupid... she thought Dunkin' Donuts was a basketball team!

Yo mama is so stupid... she tripped over a wireless phone!

Yo mama is so stupid... she bought a ticket to Xbox Live!

Yo mama is so stupid... she thought she couldn't buy a Gameboy because she is a girl!

Yo mama is so stupid... she thought a scholarship was a ship full of students!

Yo mama is so stupid... she failed a survey!

Yo mama is so stupid... she got locked in a grocery store and starved to death!

Yo mama is so stupid... she tried to throw a bird off a cliff!

Yo mama is so stupid... she took a knife to a drive-by!

Yo mama is so stupid... she got locked in Furniture World and slept on the floor.

Yo mama is so stupid... she sits on the floor and watches the couch.

Yo mama is so stupid... she stayed up all night trying to catch up on her sleep!

Yo mama is so stupid... she thought Boyz II Men was a daycare center!

Yo mama is so stupid... she threw a clock out the window to see time fly!

Yo mama is so stupid... she went to the ocean to surf the Internet!

Yo mama is so stupid... she thought the Harlem Shake was a drink!

Yo mama is so stupid... she ordered a cheeseburger without the cheese.

Yo mama is so stupid... she tried to climb Mountain Dew!

Yo mama is so stupid... that she burned down the house with a CD burner.

Yo mama is so stupid... you can hear the ocean in her head!

Yo mama is so stupid... she thought Hamburger Helper came with a friend!

Yo mama is so stupid... she got her hand stuck in a website!

Yo mama is so stupid... she sold her car for gas money.

Yo mama is so stupid... she stopped at a stop sign and waited for it to turn green.

Yo mama is so stupid... when she asked me what kind of jeans I am wearing I said, "Guess", and she said, "Levis".

Yo mama is so stupid... she thought Christmas wrap was Snoop Dogg's new song!

Yo mama is so stupid... she can't pass a blood test.

Yo mama is so stupid... she tried to commit suicide by jumping out the basement window.

Yo mama is so stupid... she got lost in a telephone booth.

Yo mama is so stupid... she stuck a phone in her butt to make a booty call!

Yo mama is so stupid... I said that drinks were on the house and she went to get a ladder!

Yo mama is so stupid... she went to a dentist to fix her Bluetooth!

Yo mama is so stupid... she went to PetSmart to take an IQ test!

Yo mama is so stupid... she went to the library to find Facebook!

Yo mama is so stupid... she stole free bread.

Yo mama is so stupid... she called me to ask me for my phone number!

Yo mama is so stupid... she worked at an M&M factory and threw out all the W's.

Yo mama is so stupid... she put lipstick on her forehead to make up her mind.

Yo mama is so stupid... it took her two hours to watch 60 seconds.

Yo mama is so lazy...

Yo mama is so lazy... she don't have dining table because she is always in bed!

Yo mama is so lazy... she stuck her head out the window to let the wind blow her nose!

Yo mama is so lazy... she was late to her "stay at home" job!

Yo mama is so lazy... her to-do list says, "Nothing!"

Yo mama is so lazy... she starved instead of getting up to get some food.

Yo mama is so lazy... she thinks a two-income family is where the man has two jobs.

Yo mama is so lazy... she arrived late at her own funeral.

Yo mama is so lazy... she stole your identity to spend more time with you!

Yo mama is so lazy... she undercooks Ramen noodles!

Yo mama is so lazy... that she came in last place in a recent snail marathon.

Yo mama is so lazy... she's got a remote control just to operate her remote control!

Yo mama is so hairy...

Yo mama is so hairy... that Bigfoot tried to take her picture!

Yo mama is so hairy... she took her shirt off and everyone thought she was a Wooly Mammoth!

Yo mama is so hairy... she has sideburns on her boobs!

Yo mama is so hairy... Bigfoot fell in love with her!

Yo mama is so hairy... her tits look like coconuts.

Yo mama is so hairy... you almost died of rug burn at birth!

Yo mama is so hairy... she wears a Nike tag on her weave so now everybody calls her Hair Jordan.

Yo mama is so hairy... it looks like she has Buckwheat in a headlock!

Yo mama is so hairy... she has tiny afros on her nipples!

Yo mama is so hairy... Harry Potter got jealous.

Yo mama is so hairy... when she moons people they turn into werewolves!

Yo mama is so hairy... she has cornrows on her back, legs, and feet!

Yo mama is so hairy... the only language she speaks is Wookie!

Yo mama is so hairy... she went to the zoo and was locked up forever!

Yo mama is so hairy... you need a lawnmower to shave her back!

Yo mama is so hairy... she was mistaken for a bear!

Yo mama is so hairy... she looks like Donkey Kong!

Yo mama is so hairy... she shaves with a weed-eater.

Yo mama is so hairy... the zoo offered to buy her kids.

Yo mama is so bald...

Yo mama is so bald... even a wig wouldn't help!

Yo mama is so bald... you can see what's on her mind.

Yo mama is so bald... everyone thought the sun was rising when she got up.

Yo mama is so bald... she braids her beard.

Yo mama is so bald... she looks like Vin Diesel's twin!

Yo mama is so bald... I rubbed her head and could see in the future!

Yo mama is so bald... Mr. Clean was jealous.

Yo mama is so bald... her hair looks like stitches!

Yo mama is so bald... you can ice skate on her head!

Yo mama is so bald... when she goes to bed her head slips off the pillow!

Yo mama is so bald... you can play air hockey on her head!

Yo mama is so bald... that she took a shower and got brainwashed.

More yo mama jokes...

Yo mama's teeth are so yellow... that when she smiles everyone sings, "I got sunshine on a cloudy day."

Yo mama's teeth are so yellow... I can't believe it's not butter.

Yo mama is in a wheelchair and says... "You ain't gonna push me around no more!"

Yo mama is so small... that she got her ear pierced and died.

Yo mama's teeth are so yellow... that when she smiles traffic slows down.

Yo mama ain't got no ears yelling... Let me hear both sides of the story!

Yo mama's house is so poor... I went to knock on her door and a roach tripped me and a rat took my wallet!

Yo mama's nose is so big... she makes Pinocchio look like a cat!

Yo mama's house is so small... that when she orders a large pizza she had to go outside to eat it.

Yo mama's head is so small... she uses a tea bag as a pillow.

Yo mama is so fat and greasy... she uses bacon strips as a bandaid!

Yo mama's feet are so big... her shoes have to have license plates!

Yo mama's mouth is so big... she speaks in surround sound.

Yo mama has so many chins... it looks like she's wearing a fat necklace!

Yo mama is so clumsy... she got tangled up in a cordless phone.

Yo mama is so nasty... her breath smells like a landfill!

Yo mama's head is so big... she has to step into her shirts.

Yo mama is so grouchy... the McDonald's she works at doesn't even serve happy meals.

Yo mama is so dirty... she went swimming and created the Dead Sea!

Yo mama is so nasty... cows with mad cow disease run from her.

Yo mama's middle name is Rambo.

Yo mama is twice the man you are!

Yo mama is so dirty... she makes dirt look clean!

Yo mama is so dirty... she brings crabs to the beach!

Yo mama is so dirty... even a carwash can't clean her!

Yo mama is so dirty... she made Right Guard turn left!

Yo mama is like the sun... you look at her to long you will go blind!

Yo mama is cross-eyed and watches TV in stereo.

Yo mama's glasses are so thick... she can see into the future.

Yo mama's house is so small... you have to go outside to change your mind.

Yo mama's feet are so scaly... you can see Crocodile Dundy in her footbath.

Yo mama's nose is so big... that her neck broke from the weight!

Yo mama's glasses are so thick... that when she looks on a map she can see people waving.

Yo mama's head is so big... it shows up on radar.

Yo mama is missing a finger and can't count past nine.

ABOUT THE AUTHOR

Jimmy Joker is the newest and most hilarious joke teller around. His jokes have made millions laugh worldwide. As a stand-up comedian and storyteller, Jimmy uses his comedy and humor to create smiles across the globe.

For more funny joke books just
search for JIMMY JOKER on Amazon

Made in the USA
Las Vegas, NV
29 November 2023

81765626R00038